# KITTENS

Anna Pollard

TREASURE PRESS

# CONTENTS

*Left:* Most people usually think of kittens as being alert, inquisitive, playful and healthy – the three kittens in the centre of this group are certainly no exception.

# INTRODUCTION

Even the biggest and most dignified of cats has at one point in its life been a kitten: an energetic youngster that chased its own tail, wrestled endlessly with its litter-mates, and tried—with varying degrees of success—to wash one paw while balancing rather unsteadily on the other three. A few weeks earlier, though, this same energetic creature was blind, weak, and completely dependent on its mother. Its consciousness was almost completely limited to sensations of warmth and cold, an empty or a full stomach.

A kitten is normally fully weaned at the age of eight weeks. During those weeks it has to learn almost all the basic skills that will ensure its survival to the age of 12 years or more: how to hunt, how to groom itself, how to fight, how (and when) to run away. It needs to learn how to behave with other cats; as all cat-owners know, the ways in which cats communicate with each other are both subtle and varied. If it is living in a domestic environment, it also needs to form a rapport with its owner.

When new-born, however, a kitten shows little immediate promise of this vast capacity for learning. In fact, it scarcely looks like a kitten at all with its tiny ears, long muzzle, and fully-extended claws, and could almost be taken for a minute puppy. Its eyes are tightly shut, its gums are pink and toothless, and it seems indifferent to noise.

For the first four or five days the kitten seems to do nothing except feed, sleep and grow. The thin tail gets thicker, the face grows broader and more catlike. But, when it is a week or so old, developments start coming thick and fast. The legs gain in strength: an eight-day-old kitten can creep with its stomach slightly raised from the ground. It then begins to learn how to groom itself (a random lick may occasionally be given to a forepaw), and most important of all, its eyes open. Some kittens – notably the Siamese – open their eyes when they are as young as two days old. As for the rest, the eyes remain shut for anything up to a week longer, with the majority of kittens taking their first unfocussed look at the world at around nine days. To begin with, kitten's eyes are a misty blue in colour and slit-like in shape; the colour will take some weeks to change, but the shape alters within days to give the kitten its distinctive wide-eyed stare.

A two-week-old kitten will often be on the brink of walking; it will also be starting to show interest in the sides of its box. By the end of three weeks, it will be walking properly – head down, toes well spread, and tail stretched out for balance. Lifted out of its basket, it will instantly head off on journeys of exploration; replaced, it will try to climb out (and, in a short time, succeed). It will investigate every object it comes across, sniffing and licking it; it will later start chewing things as well. Its claws, which have started to retract back into the paws, are less noticeable, while in contrast its ability to mew increases considerably.

In any litter there is always one kitten that is quick to develop, and one that is a laggard. It is at about this time that such differences begin to show. It is also about this time that a kitten's ceaseless shoving and scrambling among its litter-mates develops into real play.

All movements are at first carried out in extreme slow motion, and many a pounce and grab goes wide of the mark. However, co-ordination quickly improves and, by the end of the fourth week, a kitten will be spending a lot of time in mock battle. Playing with toys seems to come slightly later. The first games that kittens play are usually with a piece of string, then a paper ball, then, approaching their fifth week, with anything that moves, dangles or rustles. The obsessive exploration continues, as do the wrestling matches, but then a new dimension is added. An exploring kitten may find

A Chinchilla and her family (*right*) are resting in the sun. The colour of the kittens' eyes will soon change to the famous Chinchilla aquamarine.

a piece of newspaper that can be scrumpled, ripped, and hidden under; a fighting pair may, for instance, make their battle more interesting by sparring with each other through the gaps in an openwork laundry basket. A seven-week-old kitten – lunging, rolling over, feinting, pouncing, prancing on its hind legs is, in fact, practising all the finer points of hunting.

At seven or eight weeks, the kitten has advanced enormously from the point at which, only a month ago, it clambered out of its box for the first time. Although, of course, it must continue to be handled with great gentleness, it no longer seems so alarmingly fragile. Its claws have retracted completely, and its milk teeth have come through; both are surprisingly sharp. It can climb and land on all fours when jumping (or even falling) off furniture, for example. It can run, balance upright on its hind legs and leap over objects bigger than itself.

If all has gone well with its upbringing, it will be perfectly confident with humans and will ap-

proach them of its own accord either to play or for security. It has also learned some of the more advanced aspects of cat communication, such as the displacement wash. (The displacement wash is the token lick a perplexed cat gives itself to buy time or decrease tension.) Indeed, it is now competent at most things, except for washing itself, and may well go into an unexpected back-somersault when trying to groom its hind legs.

This growing self-reliance in grooming is vitally important to a kitten's future health. Even more important, though, is the fact that it is now on the

---

The love of and need for warmth starts early in cats. Very small kittens must keep warm in order to survive. When older, they still seek out warm places, like the tortoiseshell-and-white (*below*) lying on a sun-baked rock, and the ginger and the bi-colour (*right*) which are curled up on a bed of straw.

verge of no longer needing its mother's milk. Breeders start weaning kittens onto substitute milk food at the age of three weeks, and meat at the age of five; the mother cat, operating on her own, will wean her litter by bringing them birds and mice to show them that they are edible.

Some kittens are slow to wean, and some are fast. Some dither over baby milk, but take immediately to meat. Some dislike meat, but enjoy fish. The outcome is the same in all cases: a kitten should be totally weaned by the age of eight weeks.

Of all the milestones in a kitten's development, this is the biggest. True, there are many more to come: the departure to a new home, round about the age of three months; the development of a bond with its new owner; the growth of second teeth at five months or so, and the onset of sexual maturity, at 12 months for males and earlier – sometimes very much earlier – for females. The Siamese, always speedy developers, may come on heat at six months or even before.

The achievement of physical independence from the mother, however, is the first and most important step on the long road from kittenhood.

# EARLY DAYS

The new-born kitten is wholly dependent on its mother –
for food, for warmth, for protection, and for its upbringing.
The Siamese mother shown here has only four kittens,
while the cats overleaf have more. All of them, though,
will care for their offspring with equal devotion.

# The new-born kitten

The new-born kitten's most important needs are warmth and food. For the young Foreign Whites (*far right*) and Burmese (*below right*), the source of food is seldom far away; the tiny orphan shown below presents its rescuer with more of a problem. The very young kitten can only cope with a small amount of milk at a time, and for this reason needs feeding at frequent intervals. But a human foster-parent, however kind and determined, has to sleep sometimes and cannot provide the constant care and attention that the mother cat can provide.

All kittens, whatever their size, are equipped with the ability to suckle vigorously, and will start doing so as soon as they are born. Each

A kitten's front legs are put to another very important use when feeding. Within a day or so, a newborn kitten will develop the knack of speeding the flow of milk by pressing its mother's belly with its paws. This kneading habit – a cat's usual reaction to anything pleasurable – will stay with it for life; indeed, both the mother cats pictured will knead at their bedding because of the pleasure derived from feeding their litters. They will also purr continuously with enthusiasm.

Nursing queens (female cats) need a fair amount of extra food themselves if they are to feed their families successfully. Even so, many of them get quite thin. Apart from this, however, they often manage to look the picture of health: in spite of her large litter, the Burmese queen (*below*) has a glossy coat, shining eyes, and an alert expression. As their appetites show, the kittens are healthy, too.

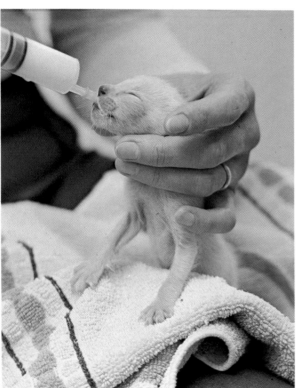

kitten will find a nipple and will attempt thereafter to suckle at the same one.

As the orphan shows, a newborn kitten's neck muscles are strong enough to support the head in a good position for suckling. In addition, its legs are stronger than they look: if it could be reunited with its family, it would instantly try to shove its way past its litter-mates at feeding time, in order to get its share of the food.

The new-born litter on the opposite page (*top right*) illustrates the saying, 'as weak as a kitten'. At this age, kittens are unable to see or walk. Within three weeks, though, they'll be up on their feet like the young Abyssinian shown above – while their mother, like the silver tabby on the right, will almost vanish under the combined weight of her extremely inquisitive and energetic kittens.

Kittens are born with their eyes tightly shut, except in rare instances. (All kittens should be kept in a subdued light for the first week or so, but this is doubly important in the case of those born with their eyes open.) Siamese kittens may open their eyes when they are only two days old, but the rest remain blind until their sixth day at the earliest. However in all cases, kitten's eyes are blue at first.

Once its eyes are open, a kitten develops very quickly. The next important milestone in its development is being able to walk and this usually occurs in the third week. The Abyssinian kitten is just reaching this stage. If it walks too fast it will instantly fall over, however, in a short while it will be moving around at a brisk, if occasionally uncertain pace.

It will also start to play with its litter-mates, just as the silver tabby kitten in the right hand picture is doing. A kitten's games are a vital part of its education: this particular kitten is both having fun and discovering how to use its legs when fighting at close quarters.

It will not be long before its neighbors stop feeding and join in the game.

The correct way for a person to pick up a kitten is the 'two hands' method: one hand is placed under the kitten's hindquarters, while the other one is placed under its chest just behind the front legs.

It is important that owners should not attempt to imitate the mother cat's technique (*right*) of picking up a kitten by the neck.

In fact cats do not carry kittens by the scruff of the neck but grasp the kittens right around the neck with their jaws. The white cat above has got a secure grip on her kitten, and will even be able to jump with it dangling from her mouth. In this case, the kitten is small enough to be held off the ground; more usually, the mother cat half lifts, half-drags her offspring to their destination.

The way to pick up a kitten is demonstrated in close-up by the tabby cat in the picture on the right. To start with, she closes her jaws round the kitten's neck, then she pulls the kitten round into the carrying position. Finally, she will drag it along the bench on which it was lying, and jump down over the side. The kitten reacts to this treatment by curling its feet up into the fetal position and relaxing its neck.

This is not the only occasion when a mother cat will take a kitten in her jaws. She will also do it when teaching her litter how to play. Frequently a grooming session for a kitten develops into a wrestling-bout, with the mother cat catching the kitten between her paws, grabbing it with her teeth, letting go, and starting all over again.

Play like this might appear extremely rough, but it is always good-natured and the kitten will emerge unscathed; indeed, it will soon follow its mother's example, with its litter-mates as victims. The straightforward tussle will develop into an elaborate game of stalk-and-pounce, while a kitten's first wild grabs are the basis on which it builds up a whole repertoire of lightening-fast paw movements.

Throughout the process, the mother cat will continue to encourage and teach her family both by playing with them and – very importantly – allowing them to play with her. Only when she is very tired will she get angry when her young kittens paw her ears and face and bite her; in fact older kittens, in addition to chasing her tail, will often use her as a springboard so as to pounce on their litter mates.

# GROWING UP

The tabby on the left has found an ideal hiding place in which to think about its next movements. The growing kitten is an ardent explorer, and its explorations can take it into the most unlikely places. An open drawer is a standing invitation to the inquisitive kitten.

# Homeground

Stone jar, drawer, or wickerwork basket – it's all one to the adventurous kittens shown in these three pictures. These ordinary household objects are, in a kitten's eyes, anything but ordinary: they are climbing frames, refuges, or anything a kitten requires it to be.
The basket, for example, can be used as both

drawer itself: it is easy to shut a kitten in by mistake – and this drawer, unlike the one on page 16, has no keyhole through which air can enter and the kitten's mews can be heard. The flex offers a different potential hazard. If the kitten gets into the habit of chewing flexes, it will sooner or later chew through one that carries a mains current. It is vital that, when kittens become confident and independent enough to explore the home, a careful watch is kept over them to ensure that they do not tamper with anything that is dangerous.

a hiding-place and a see-saw. For the kitten on top, part of the fun is staying on while its vantage-point rocks about on its handles. The kitten underneath is helping things along by clawing at the wickerwork from inside. The empty jar, though much less mobile, also makes a good starting-point for a game. It will not be easy for anyone to remove the kitten if it is determined to stay there, for even at this age a kitten's claws and teeth are surprisingly sharp and a playful swipe can quite easily draw blood!
Few kittens can resist the lure of a telephone. The coiled flex twitches at the slightest touch, and the drawers of the telephone table are usually full of pencils, paper and odds and ends. However, this kitten is in more danger than it looks. The first danger point is the

# The outside world

Most kittens, like the bi-color above, venture out into the open air at an early age. Their first experience of the outdoor world is likely to be a brief one: at the slightest unexpected noise, they go scurrying back inside. Soon, however, they will try again. To begin with, even the boldest do not stray far from the safety of the doorstep. But, as their confidence increases, they will want to explore further areas until they are quite at ease playing in any part of the garden.

As they explore, they leave behind them a whole network of kitten-sized paths and runways. They also develop distinct preferences for certain places. These, too, shift further and further away from the house as the kitten grows older; in the end, its system of 'lairs' may even extend into a neighbor's garden.

The ginger kitten opposite is extending its territory in a different direction – upwards. A kitten's climbing career starts at the age of three to four weeks when, with hind legs flailing, it succeeds in scrambling out of its box. In the fifth week, it will have begun to scale easy heights such as a sofa. Later, it will go higher still, via dining-room chairs, sideboards, table-tops and window ledges. (Windows should always be kept closed, or else guarded with screens of wire mesh; while the cat's skill at landing on its feet is legendary, a kitten's bones are fragile and are easily damaged.)

From climbing up the back of a chair, it is only a step away from climbing a tree. The ginger tree-climber may look rather apprehensive but it is, in fact, well balanced.

With hind-legs hunched beneath it, a young black-and-white prepares to pounce (*above*). Although its hunting skills are improving daily, it is still no expert at camouflage: its surroundings provide too bright a contrast, and its outline against the sky will alert all potential prey.

The trio of very young kittens (*top right*) are taking their first look at the outside world. While the kitten in the centre appears relatively calm, its litter-mate on the far right is squealing in panic. If the mother is within earshot, her kitten's cry of alarm will bring her running to the rescue.

Kittens do not only purr and growl but are quite capable of communicating by a variety of other sounds. For instance it will make one sound when looking for a toy and another when trying to get into a room, and so on. Similarly the mother cat, having a wide repertoire of sounds, can call to her kittens communicating, for example, danger or the fact that she wants to feed them.

The red and brown tabby kittens (*right*) are old enough to take the outdoor world in their stride. The red one has spotted an insect hidden in the grass. Kittens are usually fascinated by flies and spiders which they will readily play with and chase after.

# CARING FOR YOUR KITTEN

## Selecting a Kitten

There are three main ways of finding a kitten. You can go to a petshop, you can buy direct from a breeder, or you can ask your friends and neighbours if they know of any kittens in need of a home. Your local vet may also be able to help you; so might the local branch of one of the animal protection societies.

If you want a pedigree kitten you will certainly have to contact a specialist breeder or a shop. If you can, go to the breeder.

When choosing a kitten, watch the litter at play together, and avoid any that seem timid, nervous or out-of-condition. Signs of ill-health include runny noses and eyes, lank coat, and ears that are dirty.

Ask whether the kitten you choose has been inoculated against feline infectious enteritis (this can be done after the age of 10 weeks). If it has not, remember to have this done as soon as you take the kitten home.

Don't take a kitten from its mother if it is less than 10 weeks old, and never buy one on the spur of the moment. It is going to be your responsibility – and your friend – for 12 years or more.

## Feeding

Between birth and the age of three weeks, kittens live entirely on their mother's milk. (The mother needs extra food during this time.) Weaning can start at three weeks or a few days earlier if the litter is large.

Start by mixing a small quantity of substitute milk food, and placing a drop on each kitten's mouth. When they get to like it (some are slow in acquiring a taste for it), they will take it from a spoon and then from a saucer. After a week, mix some semi-solid weaning food into the milk.

Feed each kitten separately: if the whole litter is fed from a single dish, the less greedy kittens will get less than the more 'forward' kittens.

Solids – raw beef, cooked and boned white fish, cooked and boned chicken, all minced fine – can be given for the first time at five weeks, and kittens can be fed twice or even three times daily when six weeks old. Milky feeds should continue to be given twice a day.

Weaning will be over when the kittens are seven or eight weeks old: for the next few months they will need four meals a day, two of which are milk-based.

Continue with the solids described above, and introduce any new foods gradually.

Meals should be small at first, then gradually enlarged. At five months or so drop one of the milky feeds, and from now until adulthood (at nine months) kittens need three good meals a day.

Other suitable foods for kittens and young cats include cooked lamb, cooked rabbit (boned), raw liver and heart (in small quantities), canned herrings and sardines and cornflakes mixed in with other foods. All food should be cut up into long narrow strips.

Uneaten food should always be cleared away after a meal and fresh drinking water must always be available. The kitten will also need grass to chew.

One should always be very careful about suddenly giving half-grown kittens cow's milk since it may disagree with them.

## Handling

Kittens should be handled daily from birth. It is essential to check the eyelids for crustiness and also to ensure that the kitten is healthy. The kittens should be handled in the presence of the mother cat, stroking her with one hand and examining the kittens, one by one, in a quiet, calm manner, keeping them near to the mother's body. Your best way of getting kittens used to human contact is, in fact, to allow them to scramble over you whenever they want to.

When picking up a kitten, use both hands; one goes under the chest, the other under the hind legs. Hold the kitten gently, but don't allow it to wriggle free. However, if the kitten is very small, it may of course be possible to balance it quite safely in the palm of your hand, though it will, of course, very quickly outgrow this method of being picked up.

Another aspect of handling is grooming. Young kittens are groomed by their mother; you take over when they are older. Daily gentle brushing with a soft brush is essential to the kitten's health.

## General Care

Very young kittens have three basic needs: warmth, food and sleep. As they grow older, they also need exercise, playthings and a safe environment. Be sure to protect an exploring kitten from hazards like electric heaters, hot stoves and open fires. It is also vital to put guards in front of open chimneys and windows. Kittens should not be left alone for any length of time.

Apart from their feeding requirements they have a constant need for company and affection. They should be played with as often as they seem ready for it. Safe toys are cotton reels, table-tennis balls, paper tied to a length of string, and catnip mice; avoid toys made of rubber or plastic.

You should also install a scratching post, bought – if you can't make one yourself – from a pet shop. All kittens need to clean and sharpen their claws on some rough surface, for they cannot distinguish between a tree trunk and your furniture. The scratching post will save considerable damage being done to your upholstery and will be a much more effective object for the kitten to sharpen its claws on. Most kittens learn to use a litter-box before they leave their mother. Make one available when they are about four weeks old, and change the litter at least twice daily. It should be shallow enough for a kitten to negotiate, and always left in the same place. Put the kitten in it after meals until it is quite accustomed to going in there

of its own accord. Most kittens should be fully house trained after eight weeks.

A kitten in a new home needs extra care and attention for the first few days. Keep it in one room to begin with, and don't forget to give it a comfortable, draught-proof box to sleep in. Supervise a kitten carefully when it starts to venture outdoors: keep it within sight until you are confident it knows its way around. Be sure, too, to protect it from other pets until they have accepted it completely.

Kittens are trained by encouragement and – if necessary – scolding. Never slap a kitten; this is both ineffective and dangerous.

## Health

All kittens should be inoculated from the age of 10 weeks against feline infectious enteritis but only if they are in perfect health. FIE is an extremely dangerous disease, and kills nearly all cats that catch it. At the same time, ask your vet's advice about worming the kitten. Many kittens have round worms and some have tapeworms (symptoms include a pot belly, disordered appetite and lacklustre fur). Tapeworms may develop after a cat has picked up fleas. Adult cats can be treated with an insecticide, but it is extremely important that you only obtain this from your local vet.

You should also be ready to call him in if the kitten rubs its ears a lot, or looks out-of-sorts in any other way. Illnesses are often heralded by runny eyes or nose, vomiting, diarrhoea, and raised 'haws' (the inner eyelid at the inside corner of each eye). If you notice any of these danger signs, get professional help as soon as possible. If you do not intend to breed from your kitten when it reaches maturity, you should have it neutered (if a male) or spayed. Both operations, which are done under anaesthetic, can be carried out after kittens reach the age of five or six months. Neutered or spayed cats will not be able to sire or bear kittens.

# THE GOOD LIFE

At 12 weeks kittens are completely weaned and independent
although they still enjoy the ministrations of their mother.
These well grown Siamese youngsters are full of fun and
mischief, and ready to go to their permanent homes.
It is essential, however, that their new owners are aware of the
correct techniques of feeding and grooming kittens.

# Feeding

With the help of their mother – or their owner –
kittens are completely weaned from their early
milk diet at the age of seven or eight weeks.
From now onwards, their main food will be
meat, supplemented by some cereal and milk
(provided by the owner) and grass (which they
find for themselves). Grass is good for a cat's
digestion, and kittens are usually extremely
quick to discover this.

A great part of the training a kitten receives
from its mother leads up to the moment when it
makes its first kill. But although all young cats
are equipped to hunt, cat-owners naturally
prefer to ensure that they get adequate rations
from their own larder. The tabby (*left*) not only
has a satisfying meal in front of it, but a special
feeding-bowl. This, of course, is not necessary
and the kitten below makes do with an ordinary
saucer; the red long-hair on the right is enjoying
an expensive treat: a saucer of cream.

# Grooming

The first thing a mother cat does after bearing a kitten is to wash it. Her rough tongue, in addition to cleaning it, performs the same action as the slap given by the midwife to a baby – it startles the newborn infant into breathing. From that first moment onwards, washing and grooming will play a central part in a kitten's daily routine. The tabby on the left demonstrates the procedure, and is being remarkably gentle with her kitten. The mother usually holds her kitten down firmly with a paw and – ignoring

its squirming and mewing – licks it with her tongue. Very quickly, the kitten will begin to imitate her.

The kitten's first steps towards looking after itself take place when it is in its second week, and consist of no more than a dab to its stomach. Soon, though, it will get the idea, and begin to wash its front paws and stomach with reasonable thoroughness.

The back legs, however, have to wait until it has mastered the art of balancing itself on three legs and the base of the tail, a stage not reached until about the fourth week. By this time kittens will not only wash themselves but each other. They will also give a token lick to their mother, who responds in kind. (The mother will, in fact, continue to groom her family as long as they stay with her, even when they are quite capable of coping for themselves.) All that the kitten needs to acquire now is the face-washing technique (*below left and right*). Kittens seem to get the knack of doing this around their fifth week, when they are in the process of switching over from their mother's milk to semi-solid and solid food. In their early attempts to eat from a dish, their faces get thoroughly spattered, and the desire for cleanliness – now deep-seated – will not let them rest until they have got rid of the mess. As a preliminary, the white kitten (*below right*) has dampened its forepaw with its tongue; the habit extends into adulthood (*below left*).

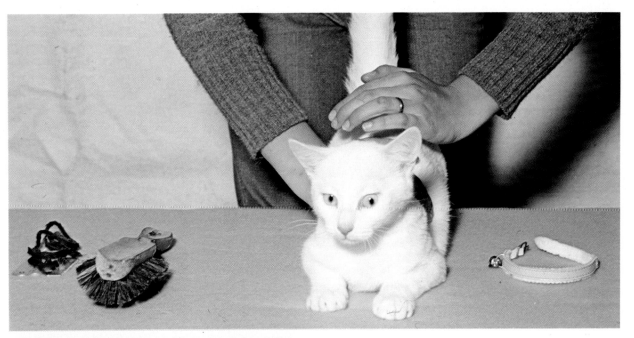

Although a kitten will be able to groom itself when it goes to its new home, it will still need help from its owner, especially if it is a long-hair like the Chinchilla shown opposite. Adult long-hairs need grooming once (if not twice) a day, and the best time for getting a cat accustomed to brush and comb sessions is when it is small. A fully-grown cat, if combed for the first time, may leave its owner in no doubt as to its displeasure!

Regular grooming is important for several reasons. It improves a kitten's looks. It gets rid of the dirt and seed-heads that all cats collect in their fur and may not be able to dislodge, as well as getting rid of the tangles. More importantly, it helps a kitten shed its loose fur; a long-hair that has to groom itself without help will lick off quantities of hair – this may accumulate in its stomach, and require an operation to remove it.

When grooming a kitten, use a soft brush for most of the work. Keep the sessions very short to begin with, and try to make the kitten feel comfortable and contented while you are working. It is, after all, accustomed to being groomed by its mother and litter-mates – it is not used to a heavy-handed human.

The second stage of the Chinchilla's grooming session gets under way. A coarse comb like the one used here (*left*) is a better choice than a fine one. After being combed, the kitten will have the fur round its neck brushed forwards to make it seem fluffier and even more attractive.

33

# THE INDEPENDENT KITTEN

Endlessly inventive, the kittens on the left have turned a basket into a look-out post from which they can watch (and perhaps catch) falling leaves. This pair's life no longer revolves entirely around their mother; at this stage, all kittens are much more interested in turning everything around them into a game. As the following pages show, they succeed almost every time.

# Play

A kitten's first toy is nearly always an ordinary bit of string. The kitten (*left*) cannot understand why it keeps moving through its paws; when the string finally pulls free, its pursuer will rear back and grab it out of the air. Then the whole game will start again. Kittens are rarely bored since they are extremely inventive and quick to improvise.

A young silver tabby prepares for flight on seeing its mother (*below left*). But it won't go further than the other side of its shelter: the idea is to creep up on its parent from behind. A mother cat will allow her kittens to play with her for hours, and – even when the kittens are growing up – will continue to initiate a game.

This tortoiseshell-and-white (*below*) appears to find the watering-can a tight fit. But, in fact, kittens love to squeeze themselves into small spaces, and are usually adept at wriggling out again.

The simplest things will amuse a kitten – and the playbox shown below is very simple indeed. All that's needed is a cardboard box, a pair of scissors, and the kitten's love of play. The kitten (*below*) is in for a shock; its opponent's next move is to dive down through the bolthole and catch its litter-mate by the hind legs – or even its tail.

Another type of playbox, which can also be a place to sleep, is shown on the right. Although only five weeks old, the occupants know all about using it as a lair and ambush-point. At the moment, the kitten on the far right is much too small to do any damage during its mock-battles, but that sideways turn of the head will be a danger-signal to watch for in the future. Many adult cats, when preparing to pounce or grab, turn their heads sideways and will probably seem charmingly kittenish until they leap into action.

football. Given a cooperative owner (and a ball that can be picked up in the mouth), they may even play at being retrievers: the owner throws the ball, the kitten brings it back, and the owner throws it again. The game only ends when the kitten decides that the ball is a mouse, and finishes it off.

If the kitten is the only pet in the home it should be given lots of toys and attended to and fussed over, so that it grows into a well-loved and contented cat. Most kittens will be very possessive towards their toys while they are playing with them and are likely to growl if another kitten approaches.

When the kitten is eight weeks old, its play gestures are like to include, increasingly, hunting and killing actions. Play both entertains and educates. It is, consequently, extremely important to play with one's kitten as often as one has the time to do so.

While a playbox – whether bought in a petshop or home-made – is an ideal toy for two kittens or more, a kitten on its own needs something with a built-in power of movement. The tabby below has found the very object: a ball. Kittens usually take a little while to get the hang of ball-games (string-games are their first favorites). But, when they do, they may play for hours on their own. First, they pat the ball, then chase it as it moves and catch it and 'kill' it as the kitten here is doing. As their skill improves, they learn to play a sort of solitary

A toy merry-go-round has everything these two Burmese kittens (*left*) could want in the way of a plaything – it moves, it rattles, it can be climbed on, sheltered under, and – given a bit of effort – pushed right over. It can even be given the occasional lick; the fact that it's a child's plaything shows that the paint is non-toxic.

Two kittens get to grips with the wheel (*below and far left*). Again, the attraction lies in the fact that the wheel moves slightly, even though the kitten's weight is nothing like enough to shift it more than a few inches when it leaps on to it. If given the chance of a real ride, both kittens would probably jump off in alarm. When older, they might well discover they enjoy transport by wagon, or toy tractor, or even by wheelbarrow. (Cats often love being trundled around in a wheelbarrow.) If they are introduced early enough to car transport, they may learn to enjoy that too, or at least tolerate it. When travelling by car it is important that all cats and kittens are housed in an escape-proof box or basket.

The escape-proof box should be large enough to enable the kitten to stand up and turn around in and it must also provide plenty of fresh air. The box ought to have a blanket in it in order to enable the kitten to sleep comfortably.

Cats are believed to be color-blind, so the young Abyssinian (*far right*) has not been attracted to the geraniums because of their bright colors. It's possible, though, that it likes the smell of the leaves. Cats often love plant smells, with the minty tang of nepeta being the first choice of most. Nepeta is also known as catnip; a soft ball stuffed with dried catnip makes a toy that few kittens can resist. Toy mice made in the same way can be found in every petshop.

The kittens shown on this page have discovered a different way of passing the time: they have raided the sewing basket. While most of its contents are dangerous to kittens and cats (especially the needles), the cotton reels discovered by the tabby below are safe, as long as it doesn't eat the thread. Old cotton reels, however, make perfect playthings and, unlike soft toys, are indestructible. For an inventive kitten, they are nearly as good as a ball.

The kittens above have tired of playing with their owner's knitting, and have turned to play-fighting with each other.

# Companions

Adult cats have a reputation – not always deserved – for walking by themselves. But kittens, in contrast, can be social animals, though their 'friends' are usually smaller than the Great Dane shown on the left.

A kitten starts learning how to behave with other animals while still very young. To begin with, its litter-mates are just so many obstacles to be crawled over (although they have their uses as a living eiderdown). By the fourth week, though, personalities have begun to emerge and the individual kitten discovers its place in the family. It may be the leader, always first to develop some new game, or it may be a follower. The entire litter, leader and led, are all subject to their mother's discipline, and while a mother cat shows enormous patience with her brood, there are limits; a kitten that goes too far will get a none-too-gentle smack.

It is also the mother who, in an unobtrusive way, determines her kittens response to the outside world. If the adult cat, for example, is unmoved by thunder, the kittens also ignore it. But if something – or someone – makes her bristle with alarm, the kittens will follow suit. It's likely that the mothers of both kittens shown here regard dogs as friends – or at least, as non-enemies.

# Exploring

There was a time when the kitten on the right hand page would have been satisfied at clambering into an armchair. It has now discovered that trees can be climbed just as easily as chairs, and are every bit as comfortable. The long-hair (*top left*) is not yet such an expert at heights, but it already has a natural gift for another type of activity; blending in with its surroundings.

The kitten's urge to explore does not diminish as it grows older; on the contrary, it takes the kitten on towards new sights, sounds, and experiences every day of its life. Sometimes the explorer seems terrified at its own daring; the tense expression of the tabby (*bottom left*) shows that it is expecting the worst to happen at any minute. It is, however, really taking a crucial step towards protecting itself. A cat – or a kitten – that has thoroughly explored its surroundings knows which places should be avoided, which sought out, and where there is a refuge in case of an emergency. Frightened though it looks at the moment, the exploring tabby would be highly upset if it were moved to the safety of the house.

Since kittens are adventurous climbers and may often climb high into the tops of a tree, it is extremely important that the owner doesn't panic. Kittens are highly sensitive and it is surprisingly easy to communicate a sense of panic. This could well excite the kitten and cause it to try and jump, whereas, left to itself, it will try and extricate itself from what appears to be the most impossible situation. If the kitten can't climb down on its own, then someone will have to climb up an extended ladder to retrieve it, and they ought to carry a zip-up bag so that they can put the kitten in it for a safe descent.

The explorations continue. Deep in the under-growth (*far left*), the adventurer has heard something that demands all its attention. It may only be an insect; on the other hand, it may be a dog, a cow, or even a car on the other side of the hedge.

The cat statue (*left*) makes less impression on this tabby kitten than a bird in the leaves below. The statue may resemble a cat, but the kitten is not deceived. In some ways, a cat's senses are far more sophisticated than ours. The five senses (sight, sound, touch, taste, smell) are all well developed. The kitten can, for example, hear the high pitched sounds of prey which are wholly inaudible to humans. It also has excellent vision, and though it cannot see in total darkness it has superb sight in subdued light.

Though kittens may well find that leaping around cars is rather exciting (*below*), there are of course many dangers. The temptation to fall asleep in the shade under a car could result in its being run over, or if it darts out into the road it could cause a car to crash in trying to avoid it.

# Stalking

The hunter below is making use of all the skills that it has been learning from infancy onwards. To begin with, its 'victims' were its littermates, and it played at stalking. But now it is entirely serious.

Up to this moment, the hub of the cartwheel has given it excellent cover for its stalk, and it will have taken immense care over the way it slid into its victim's view. Now, however, everything depends on speed and coordination. Up to a point these come naturally to a cat. Both, though are improved by practice – while the concentration of its unwavering stare has definitely had to be learnt the hard way. A young kitten is easily distracted from any game, but experience teaches it that, as far as its littermates are concerned, the game may be far from over.

A cat on the prowl likes to find a high vantage-point, and a fence is as good as anything. The watchful kitten on the opposite page is taking its bearings before setting off on the hunting-trail.

Down at ground level its companion has run a quarry to earth under a fallen log. Two choices are now open to it: it can wait, or it can give up the hunt altogether. The astonishing patience shown by a hunting cat is something else that a kitten has to learn. If it really is a talented stalker, it will settle down, tuck its tail neatly in, and prepare to wait for hours. An occasional prod with a paw will reassure it that its prey is still hiding in there – and, if the mouse does break cover, the hunt will be on again.

# BREEDS

Although the brown tabby longhair on the left and the Siamese queen overleaf are both cats, they have less in common than a non-expert might think. They represent two of the three main types of cat recognised by breeders. The third type is the domestic shorthair.
Longhairs have broad faces, small ears, shorter than average tails, and of course, longhair. Shorthairs, on the other hand, have rounded faces, 'neat' ears and short dense hair. Crossbred domestic shorthairs are commonly found in Europe and the USA.

# Siamese

Members of the best-known breed of all, the two young Siamese (*below right*) take their bearings from a tree-stump. Siamese kittens are unusual in several respects. They open their eyes earlier than any other breed. They reach maturity earlier: females may even start calling for a mate at an age when most kittens are still absorbed in play and hunting. (An owner should keep these early developers shut in until they reach adulthood at the age of nine months.) And, as shown (*left*) they are all born white. The kittens here are less than four days old; it will be another week before they develop the dark mask, ears, feet and tail of their Seal Point mother.

There are now several Siamese varieties, named according to the color of the points. In the Chocolate Point, the mask, ears, feet and tail are a true chocolate color; in the Lilac or Frost Point they are pinkish mauve. There are also breeds with blue, tabby, red, tortoiseshell or cream point. (The tortie-points, like all tortoiseshells of whatever type, are almost always female.) In each case they display the large ears, slanting eyes and wedge-shaped faces already possessed by the Siamese kittens (*bottom left*). Siamese form one small area of the foreign short hair group. Others include the Burmese, the Russian Blue, the Korak, the Abyssinian, the Havana (also called the Chestnut Brown Foreign), and the Foreign White, which looks like a Siamese with no points at all. Abyssinians come in two color varieties, brown and red, and there is also a long-haired of modified foreign-type.

# Persians

In the elegant world of the long-hair, standards of appearance are extremely high; the kitten shown above, though charming, may not in the end be red enough to convince the judges at a show that it is a prizewinner.

It will, however, make an attractive pet – and so will all white long-hairs with green eyes, tortoiseshells with blurred colours, and blacks with a couple of white hairs. According to show rules, whites must have blue or orange eyes (or one blue and one orange); tortoiseshells must show no blurring between

their patches of black, cream and red, and
blacks must be black all over. The question of
type is important, too. The pair on the left
display some of the most important long-hair
features: broad head, short nose and well-tufted
ears set wide apart.

With a few exceptions, all pedigree long-hairs
must conform to this general shape. One that
does not is the famous Turkish, or Van cat.
The Turkish has slightly shorter fur than a
typical long-hair, and bigger ears, and its face
is longer and less snub-nosed.

Another long-hair that is permitted to have nose
and ears slightly larger than usual is the Birman.
The Birman is coloured like a Siamese, except
for its paws. These are always white.

# Other breeds

Rex cats (*below*) are probably the most unusual cats ever bred. As these three kittens show, the breed belongs to the foreign short-hair group: the body and legs are slim, the face is wedge-shaped, and the ears are enormous.
But the really remarkable thing about these three tabbies is their fur. The fur of an ordinary cat consists of both a dense undercoat and silky guard-hairs. In the Rex, the guard-hairs are invisible, and the undercoat is curly rather than straight. The whiskers also show a definite curl or crinkle.
There are, in fact, two separate Rex breeds – the Devon and the Cornish. Both are named after their county of origin in England, and both arose by accident. In each case, the genetic make-up of the breed's founder-member had undergone a natural mutation. The Cornish strain is the older of the two.

The Rex can be bred in any color and breeders have been able to produce Rex cats with Siamese markings. These cats, called Si-Rex, may carry any of the Siamese point colorings now established.

All pedigree long-hairs are good-looking, but the Chinchilla (*right*) is probably the most beautiful of all. Its fur, when seen from a distance, has a sparkling, silvery look – an effect which is created by the black tip present on each snow-white hair.
Chinchillas are among the few pedigree long-hairs that are allowed to have eyes other than orange or copper. The silver tabby is another, while the white long-hair is a third.
Unfortunately, blue-eyed whites are often deaf, but this does not apply to two other blue-eyed long-hairs, the Birman and the Colorpoint.
The Colorpoint – also known as the Himalayan – looks even more like a long-haired Siamese than the Birman does, since its paws are dark. It should be thickset, like the other long-hairs, and it should have their full-faced look.

Not so much a breed as a color-type, the Agouti kittens on the left display the commonest coat pattern found in the cat world: the stripes and bars of the tabby.

The Agouti pattern is inherited from *Felis libyca*, an African member of the cat family that is usually thought to be the forefather of our domestic cats.

The gene for tabby colouring dominates all other colors, including black. Indeed, many non-tabby kittens may start life with tabby markings; this is the case with the Chinchilla, but these will disappear when the kitten grows older. In the kittens shown below, however, they are permanent – or so the owner hopes. They are both silver tabbies, and already possess some of the typical marks of the tabby. Typical marks include well-defined bars on the legs and an 'M' sign on the forehead. The kitten's eyes are still blueish, but they will change in time so that they appear either hazel or green.

According to legend, the distant ancestors of this Russian Blue (*right*) and her kittens came from the Port of Archangel in the far north of Russia. Whatever their origins, their striking colouring and beautiful coats continue to give them an exotic appearance. Although they are foreign short-hairs, their faces are not as long as that of the Siamese.

A Havana queen prepares to wash an Oriental tabby kitten (*above*). The Havana is a delightful breed incorporating all the best traits of its Siamese ancestors, but with a softer purr.

# INDEX

Page references in italics
refer to illustrations

FRONT COVER PHOTOGRAPH:
OCTOPUS GROUP/PETER
LOUGHRAN
BACK COVER PHOTOGRAPH:
OCTOPUS GROUP

This edition published in 1990 by
Treasure Press, Michelin House,
81 Fulham Road, London SW3 6RB

© 1979 Octopus Books Limited

ISBN 1 85051 486 0

Produced by Mandarin Offset
Printed in Hong Kong